# MITTENS FOR KITTENS

# MITTENS FOR KITTENS
## AND OTHER RHYMES ABOUT CATS

*Chosen by*
### Lenore Blegvad

*Illustrated by*
### Erik Blegvad

*A Margaret K. McElderry Book*

ATHENEUM 1974 NEW YORK

Library of Congress catalog card number 74-76269
ISBN 0-689-50003-3
Published simultaneously in Canada by McClelland & Stewart, Ltd.
Printed photolitho in Great Britain by
Ebenezer Baylis & Son Limited
The Trinity Press, Worcester, and London
Bound by A. Horowitz & Son/Bookbinders
Clifton, New Jersey
First Edition

The verses in this book are taken from the following sources:
*Counting Out Rhymes of Children,* Rev. Walter Gregor—"I
doot, I doot"; *The Hogarth Book of Scottish Nursery Rhymes,*
collected by Norah and William Montgomerie—"Jean, Jean,
Jean," "Lingle, lingle"; *The London Treasury of Nursery
Rhymes,* collected by J. Murray MacBain—"Mittens for kit-
tens!.," "Hush-A-Bye, baby," "A dog and a cat"; *Mother Goose's
Melodies,* Munroe and Francis—"Miss Jane"; *Nurse Love-
Child's Legacy*—"This is the cat"; *The Oxford Dictionary of
Nursery Rhymes,* edited by Iona and Peter Opie—"As I was
going to St. Ives," "A,B,C, tumble down dee," "Ding, dong,
bell," "Pussy cat, pussy cat," "Chitterabob," "Six little mice,"
"Who's that ringing?"; *The Oxford Nursery Rhyme Book,*
assembled by Iona and Peter Opie—"I love little pussy," "Three
Little Kittens," "Three young rats," "Dame Trot"; *Proverbs,
Proverbial Expressions and Popular Rhymes of Scotland,* collected by Andrew Cheviot—"Purring Song"; *The Puffin Book
of Nursery Rhymes,* gathered by Iona and Peter Opie—"Rindle,
randle," "Rat a tat tat," "There was a crooked man," "Five
little pussy cats."

## MITTENS FOR KITTENS!

Where are you going,
My little kittens?
We are going to town
To get us some mittens.
What! Mittens for kittens!
Do kittens wear mittens?
Whoever saw little kittens
    with mittens?

## AS I WAS GOING TO ST. IVES

As I was going to St. Ives,
I met a man with seven wives,
Each wife had seven sacks,
Each sack had seven cats,
Each cat had seven kits:
Kits, cats, sacks, and wives,
How many were there going to St. Ives?

Answer; only one

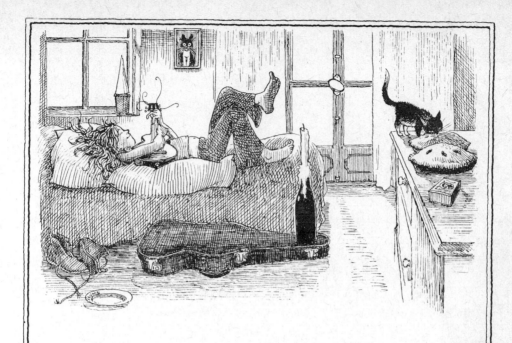

## RINDLE, RANDLE

Rindle, randle,
Light the candle,
The cat's among the pies;
No matter for that,
The cat'll get fat,
And I'm too lazy to rise.

## MISS JANE

Miss Jane had a bag,
And a mouse was in it,
She opened the bag,
He was out in a minute;
The Cat saw him jump,
And run under the table,
And the dog said, catch him, puss,
Soon as you're able.

## A, B, C, TUMBLE DOWN DEE

A, B, C, tumble down dee,
The cat's in the cupboard,
And can't see me.

## I LOVE LITTLE PUSSY

I love little pussy,
Her coat is so warm,
And if I don't hurt her
She'll do me no harm.
So I'll not pull her tail,
Nor drive her away,
But pussy and I
Very gently will play.
She shall sit by my side,
And I'll give her some food;
And pussy will love me
Because I am good.

## HUSH-A-BYE, BABY

Hush-A-Bye, baby,
Pussy's a lady,
Mousie has gone to the mill;
And if you don't cry
She'll come back by and by,
So hush-a-bye, baby, lie still.

## HODDLEY, PODDLEY

Hoddley, poddley, puddle and fogs,
Cats are to marry the poodle dogs;
Cats in blue jackets and dogs in red hats,
What will become of the mice and the rats?

## RAT A TAT TAT

Rat a tat tat, who is that?
Only grandma's pussy cat.
What do you want?
A pint of milk.
Where's your money?
In my pocket.
Where's your pocket?
I forgot it.
O you silly pussy cat!

## DING, DONG, BELL

Ding, dong, bell,
Pussy's in the well.
Who put her in?
Little Johnny Green.
Who pulled her out?
Little Tommy Stout.
What a naughty boy was that,
To try to drown poor pussy cat,
Who never did him any harm,
And killed the mice in his father's barn.

## PURRING SONG

Didrum drum,
Three threads and a thrum,
Thrum gray, thrum gray

# THREE LITTLE KITTENS

Three little kittens
They lost their mittens,
And they began to cry,
Oh, mother dear, we sadly fear
Our mittens we have lost.
What! Lost your mittens,
You naughty kittens!
Then you shall have no pie.
Mee-ow, mee-ow, mee-ow.
No, you shall have no pie.

The three little kittens,
They found their mittens,
And they began to cry,
Oh, mother dear, see here, see here,
Our mittens we have found.
Put on your mittens,
You silly kittens,
And you shall have some pie.
Purr-r, purr-r, purr-r,
Oh, let us have some pie.

## JEAN, JEAN, JEAN

Jean, Jean, Jean,
The cat's at the cream,
Supping with her forefeet,
And glowering with her een.

## THERE WAS A CROOKED MAN

There was a crooked man,
And he walked a crooked mile,
He found a crooked sixpence
Against a crooked stile;
He bought a crooked cat,
Which caught a crooked mouse,
And they all lived together
In a little crooked house.

## DAME TROT

Dame Trot and her cat
Sat down for a chat;
The Dame sat on this side
And puss sat on that.

Puss, says the Dame,
Can you catch a rat,
Or a mouse in the dark?
Purr, says the cat.

## THIS IS THE CAT

This is the Cat
That killed the Cock,
For waking her
At five o'clock.

## THREE YOUNG RATS

Three young rats with black felt hats,
Three young ducks with white straw flats,
Three young dogs with curling tails,
Three young cats with demi-veils,
Went out to walk with two young pigs
In satin vests and sorrel wigs;
But suddenly it chanced to rain
And so they all went home again.

## PUSSY CAT, PUSSY CAT

Pussy cat, pussy cat,
Where have you been?
I've been to London
To look at the queen.
Pussy cat, pussy cat,
What did you there?
I frightened a little mouse
Under her chair.

## I DOOT, I DOOT

I doot, I doot, my fire's out,
And my little dog's not at home;
I'll saddle my cat, I'll bridle my cat,
And bring my little dog home;
A hapenny pudding, a hapenny pie,
Stand ye there out by.

## FIVE LITTLE PUSSY CATS

Five little pussy cats sitting in a row,
Blue ribbons round each neck,
Fastened in a bow.
Hey pussies! Ho pussies!
Are your faces clean?
Don't you know you're sitting there
So as to be seen?

## CHITTERABOB

There was a man, and his name was Dob,
And he had a wife, and her name was Mob,
And he had a dog, and he called it Cob,
And she had a cat, called Chitterabob.
    Cob, says Dob,
    Chitterabob, says Mob.
    Cob was Dob's dog,
    Chitterabob Mob's cat.

## LINGLE, LINGLE

Lingle, lingle, lang tang,
Our cat's dead!
What did she die with?
With a sore head!
All you that kent her,
When she was alive,
Come to her burial,
Atween four and five.

## SIX LITTLE MICE

Six little mice sat down to spin;
Pussy passed by and she peeped in.
What are you doing, my little men?
Weaving coats for gentlemen.
Shall I come in and cut off your threads?
No, no, Mistress Pussy, you'd bite off our heads.
Oh, no, I'll not; I'll help you to spin.
That may be so, but you don't come in.

## A DOG AND A CAT

A dog and a cat went out together
To see some friends just out of town,
Said the cat to the dog,
"What d'ye think of the weather?"
"I think, ma'am, the rain will come down;
But don't be alarmed, for I've an umbrella
That will shelter us both,"
Said this amiable fellow.

## WHO'S THAT RINGING?

Who's that ringing
At my door bell?
A little pussy cat
That isn't very well.
Rub its little nose
With a little mutton fat,
For that's the best cure
For a little pussy cat.

398.8 Blegvad, Lenore,
BL        comp

Mittens for kittens,
and other rhymes
about cats